Food

HONEY

Louise Spilsbury

Heinemann
LIBRARY

www.heinemann.co.uk/library
Visit our website to find out more information about Heinemann Library books.

To order:
☎ Phone 44 (0) 1865 888066
📄 Send a fax to 44 (0) 1865 314091
💻 Visit the Heinemann Bookshop at www.heinemann.co.uk/library to browse our catalogue and order online.

First published in Great Britain by Heinemann Library,
Halley Court, Jordan Hill, Oxford OX2 8EJ
a division of Reed Educational and Professional Publishing Ltd.
Heinemann is a registered trademark of Reed Educational & Professional Publishing Ltd.

OXFORD MELBOURNE AUCKLAND
JOHANNESBURG BLANTYRE GABORONE
IBADAN PORTSMOUTH (NH) USA CHICAGO

Designed by Celia Floyd
Originated by Ambassador Litho Ltd
Printed by South China Printing Co in Hong Kong.

ISBN 0 431 12706 9
05 04 03 02 01
10 9 8 7 6 5 4 3 2 1

British Library Cataloguing in Publication Data
Spilsbury, Louise
    Honey. – (Food)
    1. Honey 2. Cookery (Honey)
    I. Title
    641.3'8

Acknowledgements
The Publishers would like to thank the following for permission to reproduce photographs:
Anthony Blake/John Sims p.16; Gareth Boden pp. 4, 20, 22, 23, 28, 29; Bruce Coleman /Felix Labhardt p.5, /Andy Price p.14, Kim Taylor p.6; Corbis /Pierre Colombel p.8, /Jacqui Hurst p.19, /Gianni Dagli Orti p.9, /Lynda Richardson p.15; FLPA pp.11, /D Bringard/Sunset p17; Food Features p.18; Images Colour Library p.7; National Geographic/Michael Nichols p.10; Oxford Scientific Films p.12; Photodisc p.25, /Steve Cole p.13; Tony Stone/Chris Everard, p.21, Terry Vine p.24.

Cover photograph reproduced with permission of Anthony Blake Photo Library.

Every effort has been made to contact copyright holders of any material reproduced in this book. Any omissions will be rectified in subsequent printings if notice is given to the Publisher.

CONTENTS

Words written in bold, **like this**, are explained in the Glossary.

WHAT IS HONEY?

Honey is a sweet **syrup** bees make for their food. They make honey from the **nectar** of flowering plants. Honey is also good for us to eat!

Bees mostly make honey in spring and summer when there are lots of flowers. They eat some of this honey, and keep the rest in their **nests** for winter.

bees' nest

5

KINDS OF HONEY

There are hundreds of different kinds of honey. The colour, taste and smell of different honeys depend on the kind of flowers the bees visit.

Every kind of flower has a different **scent**. When bees make honey from a particular flower, this scent becomes part of the honey.

IN THE PAST

Long ago, people collected honey from the **nests** of wild bees. This cave painting from Brazil is over 6000 years old. It shows a wild bees' nest.

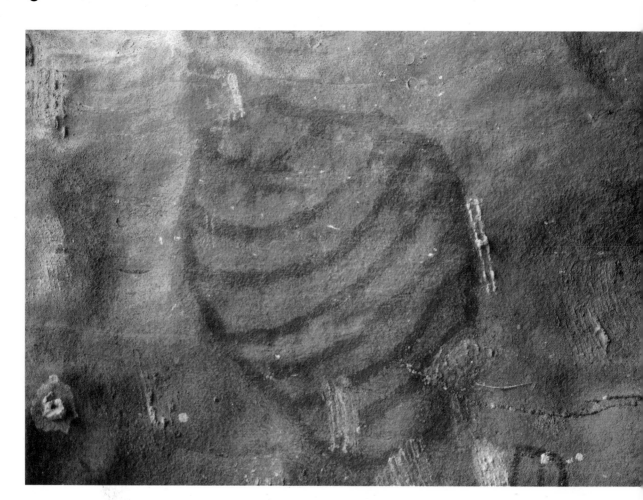

Later, people found that bees would bring their **nectar** to a nest made by humans. This is called a **hive**. This painting from France shows a woman collecting honey around 600 years ago.

AROUND THE WORLD

Pygmies still collect honey from wild bees' **nests**. Pygmies live in groups in the hot forests of Africa. This pygmy is collecting honey to share with the rest of his group.

Most honey is made on big honey farms. In America, some **producers** keep up to 300 **hives**. They fill and sell millions of jars of honey every year.

HOW BEES MAKE HONEY

Bees suck up flower **nectar** with a long **proboscis**. Back at the **hive**, they hold the **nectar** in their stomachs. This helps to turn the nectar into honey.

proboscis

Then the bees put the sticky honey into hexagonal (six-sided) **cells** made of **beeswax**. The bees put beeswax lids on these **honeycomb** cells to stop the honey coming out.

cells

BEEKEEPING

Bees make much more honey than they need. That is why **beekeepers** can take a lot of the honey for people to eat. The beekeepers keep their **hives** near fields of flowers.

Beekeepers collect the honey from late spring to early autumn. They lift the **honeycomb** frames from the hives. Beekeepers wear special clothes to protect them from bee **stings**.

TAKING THE HONEY

Before the **beekeepers** can get to the honey, they have to scrape the **beeswax** lids off the **honeycomb**. This is called uncapping.

A special machine called an extractor takes the honey out of the honeycombs. The machine spins the honeycombs around very fast to make all the honey come out.

HONEY TO US

Then the honey is passed through a **filter** to make it clear. This is like a net with tiny holes. The honey drips through the holes and any bits of **beeswax** are left in the filter.

Machines pour the **liquid** honey
into jars. Lids hold the honey in
and keep it fresh. Labels on the
jars tell **consumers** what kind of
honey is in the jar.

DIFFERENT HONEYS

You can also buy other kinds of honey. Comb honey has pieces of the **honeycomb** in it. You can eat the honeycomb as well as the honey.

Creamed honey starts as **liquid** honey. It is cooled in a special way to make it thick and creamy. You can spread creamed honey on to bread, like butter.

EATING HONEY

People eat honey on bread or toast, or as a topping for yoghurt. We also use it to sweeten cakes and breads, and even **savoury** foods.

Honey is also used in lots of the things we buy in shops. **Producers** use it in breakfast **cereals**, cakes, honey breads, mustards, and even shampoos and cough medicines.

GOOD FOR YOU

Honey is a **carbohydrate**. This means it is a kind of food that gives us **energy**. We use up energy in everything we do.

Honey also contains small amounts of **vitamins**. Vitamins are a group of **nutrients** that help to keep us healthy.

HEALTHY EATING

You need to eat different kinds of food to keep well. This food pyramid shows you how much of each different food you need.

You should eat some of the things at the bottom and in the middle of the pyramid every day.

Honey is included in the group of sweet foods at the top of the pyramid. Try not to eat too much of these sweet foods!

The food in each part of the pyramid helps your body in different ways.

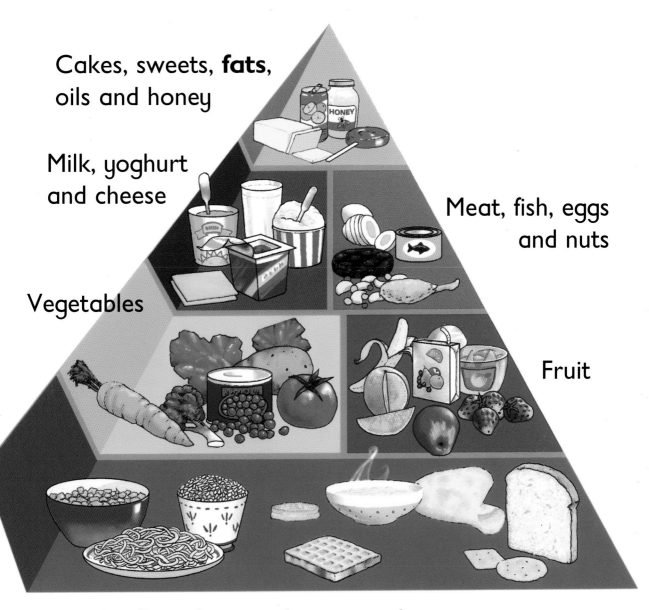

Cakes, sweets, **fats**, oils and honey

Milk, yoghurt and cheese

Vegetables

Meat, fish, eggs and nuts

Fruit

Bread, **cereals**, rice and pasta

FRUIT SMOOTHIE RECIPE

1 Cut up the banana and put the pieces into a blender with the strawberries or raspberries.

You will need:
- half a banana
- 5 strawberries or raspberries
- 225g yoghurt
- 2 teaspoons honey
- ice cubes

Ask an adult to help you!

28

2 Add the yoghurt,
  honey and the
  ice cubes.

3 Mix them together
  in the blender to
  make a smooth and
  refreshing drink.

GLOSSARY

beekeeper   person who keeps hives of bees for their honey

beeswax   special wax bees make in their bodies. They shape it to form the honeycomb. Beeswax can also be used to make candles.

carbohydrate   kind of food that gives us energy

cells   in a honeycomb, the cells are tiny boxes that bees store their honey in

cereals   breakfast foods are called cereals because they are made from cereal plants, like wheat and rice

consumers   people who buy things that they need or want, like food

energy   all living things need energy to grow. Our energy comes from the food we eat.

fats   nutrients found in some food. Butter, oil and margarine are kinds of fat. It is not healthy to eat too much fat.

filter   when something is poured through a fine mesh like a net to remove larger, unwanted bits

hives   people build hives out of wood for bees to live in and make honey in

honeycomb   group of hexagonal (six-sided) cells built by honeybees to store their honey. The cells are made of beeswax.

liquid   something you pour, like water or oil

nectar   sweet, sugary juice in the centre of a flower

nests   places bees make to live in. Honeybees make nests in tree holes or under roofs from lots of six-sided beeswax cells stuck tightly together.

nutrient   food that gives us the goodness we need to stay healthy

proboscis   part of a bee's mouth. It is long and hollow, a bit like a drinking straw.

producers   people who make or grow food or things to sell

pygmies   people who live in the hot forests of Central Africa. Pygmies live in camps in groups of about 100 people.

savoury   the opposite of sweet

scent   pleasant smell, such as the smell of a flower

sting   small dose of poison injected by bees. They only do this when they think they are in danger.

syrup   sweet, sticky liquid which is thick and runny

vitamins   group of nutrients that keep your body healthy and help you grow

MORE BOOKS TO READ:

Senses: Smelling, K. Hartley, C. Macro, P. Taylor, Heinemann Library, 2000

Plants: Flowers, Fruits and Seeds, Angela Royston, Heinemann Library, 1999

Body Wise: Why Do I feel Hungry? Sharon Cromwell, Heinemann Library

How Do Bees Make Honey? Evans Books

What's for Lunch? Honey, Franklin Watts

INDEX